WORKBOOK FOR
NIR EYAL'S
"INDISTRACTABLE"

OAK TREE READING

Copyright © 2022 Oak Tree Reading All rights reserved

No part of this book may be reproduced, or stored in a retrieval system, or transmitted in any form or by any means, electronic, mechanical, photocopying, recording, or otherwise, without express written permission of the publisher.

ISBN 9798429372822

Independently published

Cover design by: Oak Tree Reading

Printed in the United States of America

Contents

Welcome to a Better Reading Experience 5

How to Use the Workbook 6

Using this Workbook in a Group Setting 7

Pre-Reading Questions 11

Introduction Chapters 13

Part 1 19

Part 2 29

Part 3 37

Part 4 47

Part 5 55

Part 6 61

Part 7 69

Final Reflection Questions 75

Discussion Question Reference List 79

Complete Vocab List 87

Complete Key Terms List 89

Final Reflections Page 91

About The Author 93

Welcome to a Better Reading Experience

This workbook is specifically designed to optimize your learning.

By completing this workbook, you will get more value from the books you read. You will be able to easily implement the knowledge and guidance shared by authors. As a result, you will see the positive impact books start to have on your life. And most importantly, you will enjoy reading more than ever before.

Why use a workbook while you read?

When we read, we are engaging in passive learning. This type of learning results in very little retention and almost no long-term benefits. In our fast-paced, time-scarce culture we rush through books, but ironically this wastes more time, as it is almost like you never read the book to begin with.

This workbook helps you engage in **active learning**. Active learning involves participating in the learning process in some way – by writing, speaking, or doing. The more ways we engage with what we are learning, the more likely we are to remember it long-term. Even better, when you are involved in discussions with others about what you read, your retention improves further.

Lastly, you will always have this workbook available to you for an easy refresher course on the book once it's all filled out.

Here's what is included in your workbook:

- Pre-reading questions
- All discussion questions with space for writing answers
- Space to write your own summary for each chapter
- Vocabulary with space to write definitions and add words
- Key terms with space to write definitions
- Chapter reflection questions
- Final reflection questions
- A condensed list of all discussion questions and vocabulary.
- Reflection pages for writing extra notes and ideas

How to Use the Workbook

Fill out the pre-reading questions before you start.

Get in the right headspace before you start reading. Reflect on your answers each time you read.

Read each section before working on the discussion questions.

Test your retention then go back and find the answers you can't remember. This trains your brain to remember more while you read.

Define key terms.

Writing the definitions for key terms puts an extra emphasis on the most important topics included in that section. It also provides an easy guide when you want to go back to review something.

Customize the vocab list.

Expanding your vocabulary will make reading easier in the long run. If you come across a word you aren't familiar with, jot it down and you can look up the definition after.

Do the reflection questions.

These questions reinforce *why* you want to remember what you learned. Your brain will only remember information it thinks is relevant or important. Your job is to tell it why.

Return to what you wrote.

Repetition is a key to learning. Re-reading the answers you wrote a day later is a simple and very effective way to remember the material long-term.

Using this Workbook in a Group Setting

Having a reading buddy or group can be very helpful! It makes reading more fun, easily allows you to engage in the learning process, and a friend or colleague can be a great accountability partner. Let's talk about some helpful tips for using discussion questions in different group settings

Reading with Friends

Read on your own first. Becoming familiar with the material will make time spent discussing it with others much more effective.

Set goals together. Make sure you are on the same page about how much you will read and in what timeframe.

Have a plan. With busy schedules and hectic lives, committing to a regular time to meet together and discuss what you read is the only way the best of intentions aren't thwarted by life's demands.

Check-in regularly. Don't just meet up at the end of the book and expect to be able to go through the entire workbook in one sitting. Whether it's weekly, monthly or something else, find what works for you.

Talk about how you will implement what you've learned. Talking to someone about how and why you want to use the tools or information you have learned will help you not only figure out the best way to do it, but they can also help keep you on track and provide encouragement.

Be respectful. No one sees things the same way. We can learn from each other's different viewpoints. Make the discussion a safe space for sharing thoughts and ideas. If people are worried about sounding dumb or being wrong, they won't open up and you'll being doing a disservice to them and to yourself.

Reading with a Book Club

Have a plan. When you are reading with a group it is imperative you start with a plan. I recommend creating a plan for the entire book from the start. Having a set timeline and schedule will make coordination with many people much easier.

Talk about your "why". Before you begin reading, schedule a time to get together to talk about what you want to learn from the book. Discussing this with others can spark ideas, inspiration and motivation.

Divvy up the responsibility. Whether one person facilitates an entire meeting, or each person is given a chapter or section, giving someone the role of running things will help things go smoothly and take the burden off of one person. The benefit is twofold - everyone is actively engaged, and the variety will provide different perspectives and insight.

Be flexible, but stay on purpose long-term. Things never go exactly as planned when other people are involved. When this happens try not to stress out, just go with the flow. If it becomes a weekly occurrence however, it may be a good time to have another discussion about goals and why you all want to meet in the first place.

Reading With a Work Team

Get on the same page. There is likely some reason someone thought it was a good idea for your team to read this book. What is the purpose of reading this book specifically? What are your team goals? Do not start reading until you have all agreed upon this.

Set a schedule. This may be easier or more challenging depending on your work environment. Figuring out a regular time everyone can commit to is a must if you want to make the most reading together.

Set expectations. You don't want your meeting to feel controlled or contrived, but likely the meeting times are going to be shorter than a regular book club, with less time for chit-chat. Decide as a team what each person is responsible for before the meeting, during the meeting, and after the meeting. Decide what will be discussed in the meeting and what will not.

Review and adjust. After your first 3 or so meetings, take some time to discuss how everyone is feeling about the meetings. What is going well? What needs to be improved? Using a "start doing, stop doing, do more of, do less of" diagram can be very helpful for this exercise. It may also be necessary to do follow-ups until your team is happy with the process and results.

Be accountable and encouraging. You have all decided it is a good idea to read this book and that it will benefit the team as a whole and each of the members individually. Now it's time to see it in action. When you see a team member engaging in the new thing they have learned, be supportive and cheer them on. Change is hard. Having others to support you can be the difference in changing or falling back into familiar habits.

Tips for Teachers

Individual work is important, too. It is tempting to lecture straight through the material or dive right into discussions, but the way to have thoughtful, meaningful discussions is by giving students time to first read and gather their thoughts on their own.

Utilize small groups. Facilitating a discussion with 30 people (or more) can be a nightmare. Instead set up some small groups with a guided activity. Afterwards, if you think it would be helpful, send up a representative from each group to share what they discussed with the class.

Shuffle. Have people engage with different people, especially if the class is all day long or lasts for multiple sessions. This allows students an opportunity to be exposed to different perspectives and voices.

Don't try and get through everything. If you have 50 minutes, don't push your class to get through as much as possible. This takes away from the value of the questions and the ability to have an open platform for discussion. It becomes a trivial exercise in finding the answers then immediately forgetting them as soon as you walk out of the room.

Encourage collaboration outside the classroom. Ask students to work in pairs to come up with ideas on how they will apply the information they learned. There are any number of creative ways to encourage students to practice what they've learned, try out a couple ideas and see what you like best.

Oak Tree Reading Workbook

Indistractable

Nir Eyal

Pre-Reading Questions

Pre-reading questions help you clarify why you want to read this book. By assigning personal value to your reading, you will naturally remember more and begin connecting it back to your purpose. Come back to this page and review your answers each time you read to get in the right headspace.

What initially made you interested in this book? Did someone recommend it to you?

Read the publisher's summary. What appears to be the main idea or purpose of this book?

What are you hoping to gain from this book?

11

Will this book help you enhance some area of your life? Work, school, home, personal?

If you implement what the tools, strategies, or knowledge taught in the book, how do you see it being able to positively impact your life?

Jot down any other thoughts you have before you begin reading.

Oak Tree Reading Workbook

Indistractable

Nir Eyal

Introduction: _____

Chapter 1: _____

What two things does living the life we want require?

Why can't we do what we know we should do?

What is the first step to becoming indistractable?

What is the relationship between technology and distraction?

Chapter 2: _____

What are the two sides of the distraction continuum?

What is an internal trigger?

What is an external trigger?

Who was one of the earliest people to mention the problem of distraction?

What does having a wealth of information lead to?

What is required for creativity and flourishing?

What was Tantalus' true curse?

What does being indistractable mean?

What do triggers prompt?

Vocabulary

Disseminate:

Ubiquity:

_____:

Key Terms

Internal trigger:

External trigger:

Traction:

Distraction:

Chapter Summary In few sentences, describe the main concepts from these chapters.

Reflection Questions

Reflection questions take what you just learned and apply it in a meaningful way. Connecting new information with your current knowledge, experiences, and ideas reinforces the concepts and makes them more valuable to you, personally.

What did you find the most interesting in these chapters?

How does the material in these chapters relate to any of your current life experiences or situations?

What can you take away from these chapters to implement into that situation or future relevant experiences?

Was there anything that confused you or that you would like to know more about?

Was there anything you disagreed with? How would you approach it differently?

Reflections Page

Use this space for anything that comes to you as you read. It can be notes, quotes, feelings, experiences, drawings, charts, etc.

Oak Tree Reading Workbook

Indistractable

Nir Eyal

Part 1: _____

Chapter 3: _____

What is pleasure seeking activity actually motivated by?

What is at the root of all behavior?

What is the uncomfortable truth of distraction?

Why is it important to understand pain?

Chapter 4: _____

What is the only way to handle distraction?

Why are we so often discontented?

What are the 4 psychological factors that make satisfaction temporary?

What is negativity bias?

What is rumination?

What is hedonic adaptation?

What makes dissatisfaction beneficial?

What is the misguided idea about happiness?

Chapter 5: _____

What cycle perpetuates unwanted behaviors and why?

How can we manage distractions with internal triggers?

Chapter 6: _____

What method does not work when fighting distractions with internal triggers?

What are the 4 steps for overcoming an internal trigger for distraction?

What components should be noted when writing down triggers?

What is a liminal moment?

What rule can help effectively deal with distraction?

What is "surfing the urge"?

How do these techniques affect the brain?

Chapter 7: _____

What is fun?

How can difficult work be made fun?

What is fun the aftermath of?

What makes finding novelty possible?

Chapter 8: _____

What is temperament perception and how does it affect distraction?

What is ego depletion?

What have studies disproved about willpower?

What kinds of people do not show signs of ego depletion?

What controls the amount of willpower we have at any given time?

How do labels impact our outcomes?

What is the best way to talk to yourself after a setback?

What is the relationship between self-compassion and resilience?

How should we respond to the voice in our head?

What allows us to cope with uncomfortable internal triggers?

Vocabulary

Aphorism:

Solace:

Propensity:

Proximate:

_____:

Key Terms

Negativity bias:

Hedonic adaptation:

Ego depletion:

_____:

_____:

Chapter Summary In few sentences, describe the main concepts from these chapters.

Reflection Questions

What did you find the most interesting in these chapters?

How does the material in these chapters relate to any of your current life experiences or situations?

What can you take away from these chapters to implement into that situation or future relevant experiences?

Was there anything that confused you or that you would like to know more about?

Was there anything you disagreed with? How would you approach it differently?

Reflections Page

Use this space for anything that comes to you as you read. It can be notes, quotes, feelings, experiences, drawings, charts, etc.

Oak Tree Reading Workbook

Indistractable

Nir Eyal

Part 2: _____

Chapter 9: _____

What do people often squander?

What are values?

What happens when we don't make time for our values?

How do we feel when our time is not aligned with our values?

How can we use time to promote traction instead of distraction?

What happens when we don't have limitations?

Describe the process of timeboxing.

What are the two reflection questions you should ask while creating a schedule?

Chapter 10: _____

Why must self-care be at the core of the three life domains?

What shouldn't we focus on when it comes to our time?

What guarantees failure?

Chapter 11: _____

What is a residual beneficiary in a relationship?

Why must we schedule time for relationships?

What are the consequences of being socially disconnected?

What are the components of a satisfying friendship?

Chapter 12: _____

What are the benefits of work?

What does clarification at work foster?

Why does pushback occur?

How can timeboxing be used to create clarification?

Vocabulary

_____:

_____:

Key Terms

Timeboxing

_____:

_____:

Chapter Summary In few sentences, describe the main concepts from these chapters.

Reflection Questions

What did you find the most interesting in these chapters?

How does the material in these chapters relate to any of your current life experiences or situations?

What can you take away from these chapters to implement into that situation or future relevant experiences?

Was there anything that confused you or that you would like to know more about?

Was there anything you disagreed with? How would you approach it differently?

Reflections Page

Use this space for anything that comes to you as you read. It can be notes, quotes, feelings, experiences, drawings, charts, etc.

Oak Tree Reading Workbook

Indistractable

Nir Eyal

Part 3: _____

Chapter 13: _____

What is the Fogg Behavior Model?

How is motivation defined?

How is ability defined?

What is the result of being disrupted during a task?

What is the critical question to ask about external triggers?

What is the right way to think about what a trigger is?

Chapter 14: _____

What trend has led to more distractions at work?

What method can prevent distractions at work?

What do distractions lead to?

Chapter 15: _____

How much time do office workers spend on email a day?

What percentage of email time is unproductive?

Why is email a powerful draw for our attention?

What is the key to receiving fewer emails?

What is the importance of giving something time to breathe?

What is the most efficient way to process emails?

Why does tagging emails help reduce distraction in your mind?

What is the equation for reducing time spent on email?

Chapter 16: _____

When does it makes sense to use a group chat?

What are the 4 rules of using a group chat?

Chapter 17: _____

What is the wrong reason to schedule a meeting?

What is the primary objective of most meetings?

What two things must first be required of anyone calling a meeting?

When is the best time to do brainstorming?

How well do our brains absorb information when we aren't paying close attention?

What happens if screens are present in meetings?

Chapter 18: _____

What are the four steps for hacking back your cellphone?

What critical questions must be asked of external triggers?

What are three categories to organize your apps into?

What percentage of users don't adjust their phone's notification settings?

Chapter 19: _____

What causes people to perform worse on cognitive tasks?

What is attention residue?

How can we limit desktop distractions?

Chapter 20: _____

What strategy can minimize the distraction of online articles?

When doesn't multitasking work?

What is multichannel multitasking?

What is cross-modal attention?

What is temptation bundling?

Chapter 21: _____

What's the best way to hack back news feeds?

What does eliminating newsfeeds allow for?

Vocabulary

Clandestine:

Ephemeral:

Superfluous:

_____:

_____:

Key Terms

Fogg Behavioral Model

_____ :

_____ :

Chapter Summary In few sentences, describe the main concepts from these chapters.

Reflection Questions

What did you find the most interesting in these chapters?

How does the material in these chapters relate to any of your current life experiences or situations?

What can you take away from these chapters to implement into that situation or future relevant experiences?

Was there anything that confused you or that you would like to know more about?

Was there anything you disagreed with? How would you approach it differently?

Reflections Page

Use this space for anything that comes to you as you read. It can be notes, quotes, feelings, experiences, drawings, charts, etc.

Oak Tree Reading Workbook

Indistractable

Nir Eyal

Part 4: _____

Chapter 22: _____

What does becoming indistractable involve?

What is a precommitment?

What is a Ulysses pact?

Why are precommitments powerful?

When should you introduce a precommitment?

Chapter 23: _____

How do effort pacts minimize unwanted behaviors?

What are some examples of ways to create effort pacts?

Why was social pressure minimized with the use of technology at work?

What can we do to create social pressure to focus?

Chapter 24: _____

What is a price pact?

Why do price pacts work?

What is loss aversion?

What are the 4 pitfalls of price pacts to be aware of?

Chapter 25: _____

What can have a dramatic effect on our future actions?

How does self-image impact behaviors?

What is an identity pact?

How do identities empower us?

What are the benefits of secular rituals?

What reinforces our identity?

Vocabulary

Moniker:

_____:

_____:

Key Terms

Precommitment:

Effort Pact:

Price Pact:

Identity Pact:

Chapter Summary In few sentences, describe the main concepts from these chapters.

Reflection Questions

What did you find the most interesting in these chapters?

How does the material in these chapters relate to any of your current life experiences or situations?

What can you take away from these chapters to implement into that situation or future relevant experiences?

Was there anything that confused you or that you would like to know more about?

Was there anything you disagreed with? How would you approach it differently?

Reflections Page

Use this space for anything that comes to you as you read. It can be notes, quotes, feelings, experiences, drawings, charts, etc.

Oak Tree Reading Workbook

Indistractable

Nir Eyal

Part 5: _____

Chapter 26: _____

Why do employees seek distraction at work?

What two conditions cause higher rates of depression in workplaces?

What is effort-reward imbalance?

What isn't the root cause of distraction at work?

What is the cycle of responsiveness?

What is the real culprit of discomfort and therefore distraction at work?

Chapter 27: _____

What is the importance of having open dialogue?

What two things do companies consistently confuse?

What are the 5 key dynamics of a successful team?

Which of these 5 dynamics is most important?

What is psychological safety?

What occurs when there is a lack of psychological safety?

What are the three steps for creating psychological safety?

Chapter 28: _____

How does workplace culture encourage or discourage distraction?

Vocabulary

Eptiome:

_____:

_____:

Key Terms

_____:

_____:

Chapter Summary In few sentences, describe the main concepts from these chapters.

Reflection Questions

What did you find the most interesting in these chapters?

How does the material in these chapters relate to any of your current life experiences or situations?

What can you take away from these chapters to implement into that situation or future relevant experiences?

Was there anything that confused you or that you would like to know more about?

Was there anything you disagreed with? How would you approach it differently?

Reflections Page

Use this space for anything that comes to you as you read. It can be notes, quotes, feelings, experiences, drawings, charts, etc.

Oak Tree Reading Workbook

Indistractable

Nir Eyal

Part 6: _____

Chapter 29: _____

What must first be asked to allow children to develop a healthy relationship with technology?

How does the sugar-high example relate to many parents' view of how technology impacts their children?

What often follows a technological leap?

What do studies show about the use of technology on the mental health of children?

Why is technology used as a scapegoat?

Why is it important to teach our children to become indistractable?

Chapter 30: _____

What three things are needed for the human psyche to flourish?

When do kids turn to distractions?

In what way can children have autonomy over goals?

What impact do excessive school restrictions have on teenagers and children?

Why are kids drawn to their online lives?

What impact do standardized tests have on teaching practices and ultimately on children?

What do kids do when they feel that competence at school is impossible?

What is spontaneous socializing?

What hinders children's ability to socialize and play?

What is overuse of technology a symptom of?

Chapter 31: _____

What should we focus the conversation on when we talk about technology and distraction?

How can we teach children to self-regulate?

What is the reason for creating a values-based schedule with your kids?

What happens when kids are left without a clear plan?

Why is it important to get agreement from kids about them doing or not doing certain things?

How should we view failure?

Why is scheduling play time and family time necessary?

What abilities develop in children from unstructured play?

Chapter 32: _____

Why should we help our kids with external triggers?

How can we help our kids with external triggers?

Who can act as an external trigger to children?

Chapter 33: _____

What job must we teach our child to have?

Learning what skill will help kids become indistractable?

Why is discussing problems openly important?

Vocabulary

Dubious:

Punitive:

_____:

Key Terms

_____:

_____:

Chapter Summary In few sentences, describe the main concepts from these chapters.

Reflection Questions

What did you find the most interesting in these chapters?

How does the material in these chapters relate to any of your current life experiences or situations?

What can you take away from these chapters to implement into that situation or future relevant experiences?

Was there anything that confused you or that you would like to know more about?

Was there anything you disagreed with? How would you approach it differently?

Reflections Page

Use this space for anything that comes to you as you read. It can be notes, quotes, feelings, experiences, drawings, charts, etc.

Oak Tree Reading Workbook

Indistractable

Nir Eyal

Part 7: _____

Chapter 34: _____

How do other people act as external triggers?

What is a social contagion?

What are social antibodies?

What will make unhealthy behaviors socially unacceptable?

Chapter 35: _____

How can technology negatively impact intimacy?

What is the cost of distraction on intimate relationships?

What do indistractable partners do?

Vocabulary

Pernicious:

Portmanteau:

_____:

_____:

Key Terms

Social antibodies

_____:

_____:

Chapter Summary In few sentences, describe the main concepts from these chapters.

Reflection Questions

What did you find the most interesting in these chapters?

How does the material in these chapters relate to any of your current life experiences or situations?

What can you take away from these chapters to implement into that situation or future relevant experiences?

Was there anything that confused you or that you would like to know more about?

Was there anything you disagreed with? How would you approach it differently?

Reflections Page

Use this space for anything that comes to you as you read. It can be notes, quotes, feelings, experiences, drawings, charts, etc.

Oak Tree Reading Workbook

Indistractable

Nir Eyal

Final Reflection Questions

Before filling out this section, go back and reread your pre-reading questions again. When answering these questions, keep in mind your initial goal and purpose for reading this book.

What was your initial purpose for reading this book? What were you hoping to accomplish by reading it?

Did this book help you fulfil this purpose? Why or why not?

What is your next step? (For example, if it did help you, how will you implement it? If it didn't, what will you try next?)

What part(s) of this book did you enjoy the most? Why?

What part(s) of this book did you dislike? Why?

What are your top 3 to 5 key takeaways from this book?

How will you implement what you have learned into your life?

Has this book inspired you to look into other books? Which ones?

Are there any quotes from the book you would like to remember? Write them here.

Oak Tree Reading Workbook

Indistractable

Nir Eyal

All Discussion Questions

Introduction
Chapter 1

- What two things does living the life we want require?
- Why can't we do what we know we should do?
- What is the first step to becoming indistractable?
- What is the relationship between technology and distraction?

Chapter 2

- What are the two sides of the distraction continuum?
- What is an internal trigger?
- What is an external trigger?
- Who was one of the earliest people to mention the problem of distraction?
- What does having a wealth of information lead to?
- What is required for creativity and flourishing?
- What was Tantalus' true curse?
- What does being indistractable mean?
- What do triggers prompt?

Part 1
Chapter 3

- What is pleasure seeking activity actually motivated by?
- What is at the root of all behavior?
- What is the uncomfortable truth of distraction?
- Why is it important to understand pain?

Chapter 4

- What is the only way to handle distraction?
- Why are we so often discontented?

- What are the 4 psychological factors that make satisfaction temporary?
- What is negativity bias?
- What is rumination?
- What is hedonic adaptation?
- What makes dissatisfaction beneficial?
- What is the misguided idea about happiness?

Chapter 5

- What cycle perpetuates unwanted behaviors and why?
- How can we manage distractions with internal triggers?

Chapter 6

- What method does not work when fighting distractions with internal triggers?
- What are the 4 steps for overcoming an internal trigger for distraction?
- What components should be noted when writing down triggers?
- What is a liminal moment?
- What rule can help effectively deal with distraction?
- What is "surfing the urge"?
- How do these techniques affect the brain?

Chapter 7

- What is fun?
- How can difficult work be made fun?
- What is fun the aftermath of?
- What makes finding novelty possible?

Chapter 8

- What is temperament perception and how does it affect distraction?
- What is ego depletion?
- What have studies disproved about willpower?
- What kinds of people do not show signs of ego depletion?
- What controls the amount of willpower we have at any given time?
- How do labels impact our outcomes?
- What is the best way to talk to yourself after a setback?
- What is the relationship between self-compassion and resilience?
- How should we respond to the voice in our head?

- What allows us to cope with uncomfortable internal triggers?

Part 2

Chapter 9

- What do people often squander?
- What are values?
- What happens when we don't make time for our values?
- How do we feel when our time is not aligned with our values?
- How can we use time to promote traction instead of distraction?
- What happens when we don't have limitations?
- Describe the process of timeboxing.
- What are the two reflection questions you should ask while creating a schedule?

Chapter 10

- Why must self-care be at the core of the three life domains?
- What shouldn't we focus on when it comes to our time?
- What guarantees failure?

Chapter 11

- What is a residual beneficiary in a relationship?
- Why must we schedule time for relationships?
- What are the consequences of being socially disconnected?
- What are the components of a satisfying friendship?

Chapter 12

- What are the benefits of work?
- What does clarification at work foster?
- Why does pushback occur?
- How can timeboxing be used to create clarification?

Part 3

Chapter 13

- What is the Fogg Behavior Model?
- How is motivation defined?
- How is ability defined?

- What is the result of being disrupted during a task?
- What is the critical question to ask about external triggers?
- What is the right way to think about what a trigger is?

Chapter 14

- What trend has led to more distractions at work?
- What method can prevent distractions at work?
- What do distractions lead to?

Chapter 15

- How much time do office workers spend on email a day?
- What percentage of email time is unproductive?
- Why is email a powerful draw for our attention?
- What is the key to receiving fewer emails?
- What is the importance of giving something time to breathe?
- What is the most efficient way to process emails?
- Why does tagging emails help reduce distraction in your mind?
- What is the equation for reducing time spent on email?

Chapter 16

- When does it makes sense to use a group chat?
- What are the 4 rules of using a group chat?

Chapter 17

- What is the wrong reason to schedule a meeting?
- What is the primary objective of most meetings?
- What two things must first be required of anyone calling a meeting?
- When is the best time to do brainstorming?
- How well do our brains absorb information when we aren't paying close attention?
- What happens if screens are present in meetings?

Chapter 18

- What are the four steps for hacking back your cellphone?
- What critical questions must be asked of external triggers?
- What are three categories to organize your apps into?
- What percentage of users don't adjust their phone's notification settings?

Chapter 19

- What causes people to perform worse on cognitive tasks?
- What is attention residue?
- How can we limit desktop distractions?

Chapter 20

- What strategy can minimize the distraction of online articles?
- When doesn't multitasking work?
- What is multichannel multitasking?
- What is cross-modal attention?
- What is temptation bundling?

Chapter 21

- What's the best way to hack back news feeds?
- What does eliminating newsfeeds allow for?

Part 4

Chapter 22

- What does becoming indistractable involve?
- What is a precommitment?
- What is a Ulysses pact?
- Why are precommitments powerful?
- When should you introduce a precommitment?

Chapter 23

- How do effort pacts minimize unwanted behaviors?
- What are some examples of ways to create effort pacts?
- Why was social pressure minimized with the use of technology at work?
- What can we do to create social pressure to focus?

Chapter 24

- What is a price pact?
- Why do price pacts work?
- What is loss aversion?
- What are the 4 pitfalls of price pacts to be aware of?

Chapter 25

- What can have a dramatic effect on our future actions?
- How does self-image impact behaviors?
- What is an identity pact?
- How do identities empower us?
- What are the benefits of secular rituals?
- What reinforces our identity?

Part 5

Chapter 26

- Why do employees seek distraction at work?
- What two conditions cause higher rates of depression in workplaces?
- What is effort-reward imbalance?
- What isn't the root cause of distraction at work?
- What is the cycle of responsiveness?
- What is the real culprit of discomfort and therefore distraction at work?

Chapter 27

- What is the importance of having open dialogue?
- What two things do companies consistently confuse?
- What are the 5 key dynamics of a successful team?
- Which of these 5 dynamics is most important?
- What is psychological safety?
- What occurs when there is a lack of psychological safety?
- What are the three steps for creating psychological safety?

Chapter 28

- How does workplace culture encourage or discourage distraction?

Part 6

Chapter 29

- What must first be asked to allow children to develop a healthy relationship with technology?

- How does the sugar-high example relate to many parents' view of how technology impacts their children?
- What often follows a technological leap?
- What do studies show about the use of technology on the mental health of children?
- Why is technology used as a scapegoat?
- Why is it important to teach our children to become indistractable?

Chapter 30

- What three things are needed for the human psyche to flourish?
- When do kids turn to distractions?
- In what way can children have autonomy over goals?
- What impact do excessive school restrictions have on teenagers and children?
- Why are kids drawn to their online lives?
- What impact do standardized tests have on teaching practices and ultimately on children?
- What do kids do when they feel that competence at school is impossible?
- What is spontaneous socializing?
- What hinders children's ability to socialize and play?
- What is overuse of technology a symptom of?

Chapter 31

- What should we focus the conversation on when we talk about technology and distraction?
- How can we teach children to self-regulate?
- What is the reason for creating a values-based schedule with your kids?
- What happens when kids are left without a clear plan?
- Why is it important to get agreement from kids about them doing or not doing certain things?
- How should we view failure?
- Why is scheduling play time and family time necessary?
- What abilities develop in children from unstructured play?

Chapter 32

- Why should we help our kids with external triggers?
- How can we help our kids with external triggers?
- Who can act as an external trigger to children?

Chapter 33

- What job must we teach our child to have?
- Learning what skill will help kids become indistractable?
- Why is discussing problems openly important?

Part 7

Chapter 34

- How do other people act as external triggers?
- What is a social contagion?
- What are social antibodies?
- What will make unhealthy behaviors socially unacceptable?

Chapter 35

- How can technology negatively impact intimacy?
- What is the cost of distraction on intimate relationships?
- What do indistractable partners do?

Oak Tree Reading Workbook

Indistractable

Nir Eyal

Complete Vocab List

Aphorism

Clandestine

Disseminate

Dubious

Ephemeral

Epitome

Moniker

Pernicious

Portmanteau

Propensity

Proximate

Punitive

Solace

Superfluous

Ubiquity

Oak Tree Reading Workbook

Indistractable

Nir Eyal

Complete Key Terms List

Distraction

Effort Pact

Ego depletion

External trigger

Fogg Behaviors Model

Hedonic adaptation

Identity Pact

Internal trigger

Negativity bias

Precommitment

Price Pact

Social antibodies

Timeboxing

Traction

Final Reflections Page

Use this space to write out your final thoughts, opinions, ideas, or feelings about your experience reading this book. This will help you later when you want a refresher on the material.

We hope you found this resource useful and look forward to helping you again soon for your next read.

About The Author

Oak Tree Reading creates comprehensive workbooks for your favorite non-fiction books. Primary genres include self-help, communication, relationships, and professional skills.

Our workbooks have been carefully designed to optimize learning. This allows you to get the most from what you are reading.

Read with friends. Our workbooks are perfect for facilitating meaningful discussions in any type of group setting. They are a great resource for educators, as well. Try it out! Soon you won't want to read any other way.

Sign up for our newsletter for updates on the latest releases at https://www.oaktreereading.com.

We Love Feedback!

Our mission is help you get the most value out of any book you read. Help us help you! What did you like? What would you change? Are you a student, a parent, a manager? How did this workbook help you? Please share your experience with us so we can keep making it better!

You can leave a review or visit our website to get in touch.

We appreciate your support!

Made in the USA
Monee, IL
27 May 2023

34766107R00056